Plan to Write a Book about Life Insurance According to Biblical Principles

Introduction: Life Insurance – Why We Need it

Biblical references to God's Expectations of Parents

I.   The Duty to Support and Protect the Family
II.   God's Blessings for Obedience
III.   Planning for One's Financial Future
IV.   Budgeting for Life Insurance
V.   College Funding Options
VI.   Retirement Options
VII.   Storing Important Records
VIII.   Women as Heads of Household – Changing the Tide
IX.   The Needs of Divorced Women
X.   The Needs of Single Women
XI.   The Needs of Widows
XII.   Dispersing the Life Insurance Funds
XIII.   Business Insurance

Life Insurance: A Biblical View

By Gail Cavanaugh

Introduction

Is Life Insurance Biblical?

Because of the unsavory and unethical practices of a few financial services and banking representatives, many people do not trust the systems which these industries have initiated to assist people in managing their finances. The life insurance industry is one such institution.

First of all, no one likes talking about life insurance or matters of death, but it is something that we will all face at some point in our lives. Insurance is an age old solution to a problem with suffering losses in the event of a catastrophe. The idea is to minimize losses by passing on the risk to someone else who can pay for the loss when it occurs.

The Babylonians and Chinese were the first to consider the losses which they incurred while shipping their goods across the high seas. Because accidents were prevalent due to capsizing, the merchants spread their shipments among several carriers to minimize their losses. They would also pay an additional fee when they received a loan to transport the goods, as a guarantee that the lender would cancel the loan if the merchants suffered any losses.

Around 600 B.C., the Greeks and Romans started offering benefits for the families of deceased members of their benevolent societies and paid for funeral expenses for the society members. In England, in

the Middle Ages, these societies were known as "guilds" and "friendly societies." Health and life insurance, however were not formally established until the 1700s.

Throughout history, mankind has had a need to protect their families and their businesses from financial calamity. Life insurance was created to help mitigate those losses. This book explores the Biblical view of life insurance and how it impacts the families.

As Christians, God expects us to provide for our families and to take responsibility for them. We read in I Timothy 5:8, "But if any provide not for his own, and especially for those of his own house, he hath denied the faith, and is worse than an infidel." God makes it very clear here that the husband should provide for his family.
http://www.allaboutgod.com/role-of-husband-in-the-bible.htm

Further, God considers the man who provides for his family and his descendants a righteous man. Proverbs 13:22 says, "A good man leaveth an inheritance to his children's children: and the wealth of the sinner is laid up for the just." Psalm 112:1 "Praise ye the Lord. Blessed is the man that feareth the Lord, that delighteth greatly in his commandments. His seed shall be mighty upon the earth; the generation of the upright shall be blessed."

I Peter 3:7 says, "Husbands, in the same way be considerate as you live with your wives, and treat them with respect as the weaker partner and as heirs with you of the gracious gift of life, so that nothing will hinder your prayers." Here God is stressing that the husband be considerate of the wife and to treat the wife as the weaker partner. If the husband is to provide for the wife, then the wife would be at a loss if he was to die prematurely. Therefore, by providing her with life insurance, he is being considerate to ensure that her needs will continue to be met after he expires.

This assumes, however, that the husband is gainfully employed. The reality is that not all husbands today are gainfully employed, nor are all of the husbands living with their families. Natasha Cornelius states in her July 7, 2015 blog post that "nearly 44% of the women in the household are the primary breadwinners."
https://www.quotacy.com/womens-need-for-life-insurance/

Because of the opportunities for career advancement for women, this figure has been increasing since the early 1990's to its current level today. http://www.elle.com/culture/career-politics/a11880/women-the-new-breadwinners-632791/

Accordingly, it now appears that the women need more life insurance on themselves because their children and husbands are now dependent on them financially, in some cases.

Women have an obligation to provide for their families because of the increases in their responsibilities and in their incomes. I Timothy 5:8 applies to everyone. However, it is also clear that the husbands are not taking their rightful place as providers of the family, according to the Bible. In some cases, this is due to circumstances beyond their control and in other cases it is due to a defect in their character which prevents the men from owning up to their responsibility. The man who takes responsibility for his family will be blessed. Psalm 112:3 says, "Wealth and riches shall be in his house: and his righteousness endureth forever."

Life insurance is a way for God to provide for our needs according to Philippians 4:19, "But my God shall supply all your need according to his riches in glory by Christ Jesus."

These truths are written in the Bible to encourage Christians. We read theses passages time and time again, but unfortunately we do not know how to apply them to our lives. Hopefully, reading this book will give some insight on how God has provided a plan for families to be protected.

Chapter One

The Duty to Support and Protect the Family

Much has been written about life insurance and the parent's responsibility to protect the family. God created the institution of marriage and the family so that the man would not be alone. God created the woman as the man's helpmate and the man was assigned to protect and support the woman and their children.

God gave man a great responsibility as ruler over all that he created. With that responsibility, God has given man a set of precepts to follow in order to be successful and to fulfill the needs of the family. He gave man physical strength and made woman the weaker one because she lacks the physical strength that men have. In the days that God created man and woman, man needed the physical strength to protect the woman from predators.

This is still true today as the wife looks to the husband to protect her from harm in the form of aggression against her, whether they be physical, emotional, or the threat of theft or abuse. When the woman turns to her husband for help, she is responding to God's mandate for the man to protect the woman.

God said to Adam, "Because thou hast hearkened unto the voice of thy wife, and hast eaten of the tree of which I commanded thee, saying, 'Thou shalt not eat of it,' cursed is the ground for thy sake; in sorrow shalt thou eat of it all the days of thy life," Genesis 3:17. From that day forward, man and woman had to endure hardship as a result of their disobedience to God's commands in the Garden of Eden.

Because of the man's and woman's sin in the Garden of Eden, man was to have ruler ship over the woman because Satan tempted her. This is also confirmed in 1 Corinthians 11:3 which says, "But I want you to understand that Christ is the head of every man, and the man is the head of a woman, and God is the head of Christ." Since man is to be the head of every woman, it is his obligation to bring money into the house.

The man had to do this because of his sin in the Garden of Eden: "Then to Adam He said, "Because you have heeded the voice of your wife, and have eaten from the tree of which I commanded you, saying, 'You shall not eat of it': "Cursed is the ground for your sake; In toil you shall eat of it all the days of your life." Now, man has to work hard each day of his life.

When man was the only bread winner in the family, before 1960, this is what he did. He had a job when he met the woman and then provided for her and the children when she began to give birth to their children. He worked his entire life until he retired.

Until the 1960's, for the most part, man was always the breadwinner of the family, while the wife stayed at home and cared for the children. The man found a job and spent many years working at the same employer until he retired.

I Peter 3:7 says, "Husbands, in the same way be considerate as you live with your wives, and treat them with respect as the weaker partner and as heirs with you of the gracious gift of life, so that nothing will hinder your prayers."

Here God is stressing that the husband be considerate of the wife and to treat the wife as the weaker partner. If the husband is to provide for the wife, then the wife would be at a loss if he was to die prematurely. Therefore, by providing her with life insurance, he is being considerate to ensure that her needs will continue to be met after he expires.

This assumes, however, that the husband is gainfully employed. The reality is that not all husbands today are gainfully employed, nor are all the husbands living with their families. Natasha Cornelius states in her July 7, 2015 blog post that "nearly 44% of the women in the household are the primary breadwinners."
https://www.quotacy.com/womens-need-for-life-insurance/

Because of the opportunities for career advancement for women, this figure has been increasing since the early 1990's to its current level today. http://www.elle.com/culture/career-politics/a11880/women-the-new-breadwinners-632791/

Accordingly, it now appears that the women need more life insurance on themselves because their children and husbands are now dependent on them financially, in some cases.

Women have an obligation to provide for their families because of the increases in their responsibilities and in their incomes. I Timothy 5:8 applies to everyone. Life insurance is a way for God to provide for our needs according to Philippians 4:19, "But my God shall supply all your need according to his riches in glory by Christ Jesus."

These truths are written in the Bible to encourage Christians. We read theses passages time and time again, however, we do not know how to apply them to our lives. Hopefully, reading this book will give some insight on how God has provided a plan for families to be protected.

Many opportunities have been available for women since the 1960's, and as such, the women are now assuming the responsibility to protect and provide for the families. As a result, the families are "not so nuclear" anymore. About forty percent of the children in the United States live in female headed households.

Women have been trying to create ways to enter the job force since the days of Prohibition in the United States, in the mid 1800's. They have now entered the workforce in large numbers. Many of them hold jobs which only men traditionally held.

There are several groups of women in the United States today who have a need to understand how to protect their incomes and how to plan for the future. These women include:

Seniors: The seniors aged 50 to 85 may need final expense benefits for themselves and may want to purchase life insurance on their grand - children. Some may have a term policy they may need to convert to permanent coverage. If they recently sold a house, they may want to transfer the money into an annuity to earn interest on the money, rather than to deposit the funds into a bank.

Finding a life insurance agent which one can trust may be a challenge because of the times that we are living in. Many people find it difficult to trust people in the financial services industry because of the recent experiences with the Economic Crisis of 2008, where many people lost money in the stock market crash due to the dishonest behavior of Bernie Madoff.

It is important to work with someone that you can trust. One way is to seek referrals from friends or family. If they have had a good experience with someone, then it would be to your advantage to engage in his/her services as well. This is especially true if the amount of money you would like to discuss is substantial.

The qualities that one should search for are honesty, integrity, knowledgeable, consideration, and compassion. A person with these qualities will take the time to make sure that things are done correctly. This would be a person with a reputation such as Job, who "fears God and turns away from evil," Job 2:3.

This person would not be tempted to act in a way which is not in the client's best interest. The person would do a financial needs analysis to determine the goals, the needs, and the client's budget to create the plan for financial security.

The insurance agent or financial services representative would not consider his own interests, but the interests of the client would come first. Philippians 2:3 – "Do nothing out of selfish- ambition or vain conceit, but in humility, consider others better than yourselves."

The competent insurance agent has the attitude of a servant, as Christ did in Matthew 20:26-28, "It shall not be so among you. But whoever would be great among you must be your servant, and whoever would be first among you must be your slave, even as the Son of Man came not to be served but to serve, and to give his life as a ransom for many."

Unfortunately, some financial services representatives who lack the training to be able to have an attitude of service toward the clients. Consumers must be aware of this and act accordingly. If the agent is too anxious to take your application before he/she has done a

thorough work on your case, it would be wise to refrain from acting too quickly, lest the agent make an erroneous decision about your circumstances. Proverbs 14:29 says, "He that is hasty of spirit exalteth folly." The Bible Topix blog includes this definition, "Haste is quickness; hurry; an over eagerness to act; rashness. Rashness is unwise haste; recklessness; a response without due deliberation (prayerfulness and forethought) or caution."
http://bibletopix.blogspot.com/2012/06/haste-rashness.html

If an agent in haste, there is a tendency to make mistakes, erroneous conclusions, and inappropriate decisions for your circumstances. A life insurance agent must give careful consideration to your needs, and if the agent is a Christian, decisions should be made thoughtfully and prayerfully. There is always time to do things with careful forethought.

At times, the client may be the one who seeks a quick solution to his/her problem. If the agent is aware of this, he/she will take the time to explain to the client how to proceed and why it is in the best interest of the client to cooperate with the agent in allowing him/her to make the right decisions. In doing so, the insurance agent is

"speaking, not to please man, but to please God who tests our hearts," I Thessalonians 2:4. God will test the insurance agent to determine how he makes decisions and whether they are lining up with His word.

The insurance agent should be honest with the client so as not to give him/her erroneous conclusions about his/her application. For instance, at times, agents meet clients who have illnesses or a less than favorable health history. Today, this is more common than we think. If there is a possibility that the client could be rated because of his/her health history, the agent should let the client know. It is better to be truthful than to give the client false hope. Many clients have been disappointed because they were led to believe the company would offer them a policy, only to find out that their health history was too risky.

By the same token, the client should be truthful to the agent, as it would help the agent to determine which company to which to assign the policy. Many agents have been surprised to learn that a company declined to write a policy for their client because of the extensive or severe health history. The client failed to notify the agent fearing that he/she would be declined. There was a time years ago when certain

health conditions were considered too great a risk for the insurance companies to assume, however, there are insurance companies who will assume these risks.

If the agent explains the decision-making process carefully, and encourages the client to be honest about his/her health, then the

insurance agent is in a better position to assist the client in securing an offer from the insurance company. Many companies are more willing to assume risks which, in the past, they would not assume. Therefore, it is in the client's best interest to be honest about their health history.

A knowledgeable life insurance agent has had many experiences in writing and submitting applications to the company. He/she is in the best frame of mind to take and submit the applications to the company. If he/she is an independent agent, he/she has several options for the client based on their needs and health history,

Retirees- Those who are retiring or downsizing may need to rollover their retirement accounts to an annuity to start monthly payments to supplement their pensions or social security. They may also have CDs

that they may want to rollover into an annuity, depending on the interest rates. They would also want to review their life insurance policies to ensure their families are adequately protected and they the retiree has enough income to live on. If not, withdrawing cash from the life insurance policy may be an option.

Divorced Women: Divorced women need to replace their life insurance. Often, they were included under a rider on the husband's life insurance policy and he may not want to continue paying for her life insurance coverage. The wife may have a desire to have her own

policy with another company, to be free of the past. She may also have been awarded a share of retirement plans, pensions, and other cash assets which need to be transferred to an annuity or other type of savings vehicle.

If the wife has custody of the children, she may need to increase the value of her life insurance policy, since she now is the breadwinner, regardless of the husband's contribution.

Widows - Widows need help in organizing their financial records after the death of their husband, and in taking steps to collect the benefits they are entitled to receive.

If the husband handled the financial matters, the widow needs to be educated about her benefits as well as assistance inorganizing the payments she will receive as death benefits. She will have to determine if she has enough to live on and to plan a budget for her expenses.

Women of Influence – Affluent women who are heads of household and make more money than their husbands. They are now in charge of the finances and may lack the knowledge to plan their financial security. They may not have time to sit down and plan their finances,

They hesitate seek the help of a financial advisor because they struggle with relating to them. Yet many women have a fear that they will outlive their money or that they will become homeless women.

These women will need the help of someone whom they feel they can relate to and someone they can trust. Many of the women do not understand financial matters nor life insurance and will feel vey intimidated about making plans. The life insurance agent will have to be very patient with these women.

Single Women – heads of households with children. This group includes women who are working, divorced, single heads of household, widows, same-sex marriages, and women of influence. They often attend workshops to gain a better understanding of how to manage their finances. About seventy percent of single mothers do not have life insurance. https://smartasset.com/life-insurance/how-much-life-insurance-do-single-parents-need

To be successful, the material must be presented in a way that women will understand it. There is a concern among women that marketing materials are too complex and more geared toward men.

Women are more comfortable in a social setting and need financial representatives who understand and care about their needs. They benefit from meeting and relating to other women with the same problems and issues.

Although this is a relevant concern among women, the life insurance agent should exercise care in not devaluing their services. Insurance is a highly paid profession and the women need to understand this position. The services that a woman receives from a competent agent are well worth the fees that life insurance agents receive.

If the women feel the fees are too high, they will likely research the Internet for articles on life insurance and decide to make their own decisions about life insurance for their families. Then they will shop around for the lowest price, regardless of the claims paying ability of the companies or the financial strength of the insurance companies. They will even call agents asking them questions about life insurance and the policies and then call a few other companies to compare notes. They will decide on a company from this research.

If the agent attempts to show them the error of their ways, they will probably not listen because they feel they have made the right decision. The Bible describes these types of individuals as "proud scorners." Proverbs 28:25 says, "He that is of a proud heart stirreth up strife: but he that putteth his trust in the Lord shall be made fat."

Because the proud scorner does not have a relationship with the Lord, they will not even consider that God has a better solution. The proud scorner will choose to exercise their free will at the expense of making a bad decision, because God has given us that option. They would rather do things their own way. Proverbs 13:16 says, "Every prudent man dealeth with knowledge: but a fool layeth open his folly."

These women are making their decisions without the help of God or godly counsel. The Bible says, "Where no counsel is, the people fall, but in the multitude of counselors, there is safety." It is a good idea to search the Internet for answers, but life insurance and financial matters are such a complex topic to research, that it would be advisable for women to discuss their findings with a competent financial expert.

People who work in the financial field have spent a great many years acquiring their knowledge. It is impossible to have a complete understanding of life insurance in a matter of a few hours.

Additionally, most people who conduct research on the Internet about life insurance do not know the issues well enough to search for them. If you try to explain that to them, they may get indignant and insist they have done the required amount of research. Proverbs 21:24 says, "Proud and haughty scorner is his name, who dealeth in proud wrath."

Most life insurance agents have been trained to make the best decisions and recommendations for their clients. The life insurance industry is a highly regulated field which requires every life insurance agent to take continuing education courses yearly. They learn how to make the best decisions for their clients as well as how to conduct themselves in an ethical manner.

God chose them for this position because of their understanding of financial matters and their willingness to exercise wisdom in managing people. If they have been in the business long enough, they have had to make decisions for hundreds, and in some cases, thousands of individuals. They know what works and what will cause failure. They practice "counsel and sound judgement," and they have "understanding and strength," Proverbs 8:14.

If the women spend their time researching the insurance agents with others, going to the Lord for guidance, and getting to know the agents, they will find the right one who can meet their needs. Proverbs 1:5 says," A wise man will hear, and will increase learning and a man of understanding shall attain unto wise counsels." The woman who practices folly will never gain an understanding of the life insurance field nor will she seek wise counsel. Instead, she will rely on what she has learned through the Internet alone.

Chapter Two

God's Blessings for Obedience

Because God is a loving God, he has given us mandates for supporting and protecting the family as well as rewards or blessings for being obedient to his commands. However, unless Christians grew up in a household where parents taught this knowledge, they may not be aware of it.

1 Kings 2:3 says, "Observe what the Lord your God requires: Walk in obedience to him, and keep his decrees and commands, his laws and regulations, as written in the Law of Moses. Do this so that you may prosper in all you do and wherever you go."

Mankind needs guidance from the Lord in his day to day affairs. People are not perfect and do not have all the answers. Therefore, God sent his Son, Jesus to be a Savior of the world. We needed salvation from our life of destruction, characterized by making the wrong decisions. In Christ, we have a perfect solution to our problems. We can consult the Bible for answers or go to the Lord in prayer.

God makes it clear in this verse that he will bless us for being obedient. There are many examples in the Bible of people who were blessed for being obedient to the Lord's commands.

Noah spent years building an ark in accordance with God's commands and in return, his family was saved from a great deluge. "By faith Noah, being warned by God concerning events as yet unseen, in reverent fear constructed an ark for the saving of his household. By this he condemned the world and became an heir of the righteousness that comes by faith," Hebrews 11:7.

It takes great faith to obey a command of the Lord which we do not understand. But, doing so results in great rewards. Noah had a relationship with God and because of this relationship, he could trust

and obey God. Genesis 6:9 says, "Noah was a just man and perfect in his generations, and Noah walked with God."

God had become upset with the results of allowing the Sons of God to be mated with the daughters of men. Their offspring became giants on the earth and their thoughts were evil. Therefore, God wanted to

destroy them. He had Noah build an ark which would transport his family and some animals during a deluge which God create. Noah built the ark, it rained for forty days and forty nights and Noah and his family were saved, while mankind was destroyed.

 Abraham and Isaac were obedient father and son in the Bible. Isaac was the son of Abraham, born to him at an advanced age. God gave Abraham a son in old age as his wife, Sarah, was not able to bear children. Isaac brought up Isaac in accordance with the law of God and taught Isaac the importance of obedience to God.

God tested Abraham and commanded him to offer his son Isaac as a sacrifice on the altar. Although Abraham was very upset about this, he went to the place where God told him to go and offered his son and began to tie him down to offer as a sacrifice. As Abraham was preparing Isaac for the sacrifice, an angel of God told Abraham to stop. Because he was being obedient to God, God stopped him from sacrificing his son and ordered Abraham to let the son go. Thus, God blessed Abraham with descendants "as numerous as the stars." Abraham became the father of many nations. God said in Genesis 22:17, "I will surely bless you and make your descendants as

numerous as the stars in the sky and as the sand on the seashore. Your descendants will take possession of the cities of their enemies, and through your offspring all nations on earth will be blessed, because you have obeyed me."

Because Isaac obeyed his father, he was blessed with a long life of prosperity. Genesis 25:11 "After Abraham's death, God blessed his son Isaac, who then lived near Beer Lahai Roi." Genesis 35:28 Isaac lived a hundred and eighty years."

Joshua was one of the men who was chosen to search out the land of Canaan for the Israelites. This was the promised land that they were to take for their blessing from the Lord. Joshua and Caleb went into a mountain and looked down on Canaan to see what kind of land it was. Moses wanted to know the condition of the land before the Israelites took possession of it.

He wanted to know whether the people were weak or strong, how they lived, in tents or strongholds, whether the land was good and whether there was any wood there. Was a land flowing with milk and honey. The people were strong and the city was well protected. Caleb suggested that they go in and take over the city.

They discovered that the land. However, the men that went into the land with Joshua and Caleb were afraid that they would not be able to take over the city because they were outnumbered. They gave a bad report to the Israelites when they came back.

David

Job

Mary

Peter

John

Rahab

Ruth

Esther

Deborah

Elizabeth

Daniel

Chapter Three

Planning One's Financial Future

Planning one's future involves conducting an examination of one's lifestyle to determine the amount of money one needs to live on at some point in time in the future. It would involve securing a financial needs analysis to determine if the person and family will be able to live their chosen lifestyle at some future date.

Jeremiah 29: 11 says, "For I know the plans I have for you, declares the Lord; plans to prosper you and not to harm you; plans to give you a hope and a future." Our plans will succeed, if we turn them over to the Lord. He knows what we want and desire. The consumer would need an expert, such as a life insurance agent or financial planner to help set the financial goals and determine where and how to accumulate the money the consumer would need to live.

If one is shopping around for life insurance, no doubt they have discovered the many possibilities and so many companies to choose from. But, how do you know you are choosing the best company?

There are two avenues to pursue in choosing the right life insurance agent. You can choose to do business directly with an insurance company representative who represents, one company or you can choose an independent agent who represents several companies.

An insurance company representative is limited to offer the products that are sold only with the insurance company who employs him/her. Often, if the product is not suitable for the situation, one must shop around for another company. A consumer may end up shopping around for many companies before finding the right one. Because some of the decisions will involve complex issues, one could make the wrong decision involving your family, if an insurance agent is not involved in making the decision.

On the other hand, an independent agent may assist consumers in choosing the best product among the many companies he/she represents. Since an independent agent may represent several companies, he is skilled in finding the right product for the family. There are more choices to consider, and more benefits to acquire. Also, the agent can choose more than one product from different companies which can meet your needs.

LIMRA has determined that there are two reasons why people do not buy life insurance, even though they need it. Most of the Gen X and Gen Y families who need the life insurance fail to purchase it because of the other needs which their budgets dictate or because they feel they cannot afford it. Because of the new digital products that are on the market, people place a priority on purchasing these products and the membership fees to subscribe to the service first. Often, there is little or no money left to buy insurance. LIMRA publishes a **Facts About Life Sheet** every year for Life Insurance Awareness Month. The 2016 report is printed in Appendix A in the back of this book.

The advantage to having an independent insurance agent is that he /she represents several companies, not just one. He/she can offer a variety of products in attempting to search for a product to meet the immediate need for insurance. For example, most companies have several life insurance products, including a term, whole life, and a universal life policy which can provide mortgage insurance, final expense benefits, or a supplement to a savings or retirement plan.

Many of the major insurance carriers offer group benefits in addition to the individual policies offered to families. In some cases, family members who are operating businesses would have an opportunity to explore the many policies which could meet the needs of their employees as well as their business partners. These valuable group benefits would enable the business owner to attract valuable employees by offering a more competitive benefits program. Unlike the insurance agents who work for the major insurance carriers, there are many options from which to choose.

By having these many options to choose from, heads of households and companies can receive valuable guidance in choosing the best life insurance coverage for the family from an independent agent.

Finding a solution to your financial security needs takes time and patience. Insurance professionals spend many years completing continuing education requirements to keep abreast of the current trends and changes in the laws. In this way, they can be better informed to address the needs of the consumers.

Financial security for families is very crucial considering the current state of the economy. It is important to address these needs as early as possible to cut down on the high costs and to prevent the family from suffering financial calamity due to poor planning. When families are financially secure, the children are happier, healthier, and avoid the social problems caused by parents who are stressed because they have no way of providing for the financial security of their children.

Life insurance agents can help alleviate the stresses that the families experience, especially due to the economic conditions of this country.

A life insurance plan could provide solutions to many needs including college funding, estate planning, retirement, and business continuity. No matter what your needs are, there is an affordable life insurance policy which could address that need for your financial security.

Since most families cannot address all their needs at once, the planning can be done in stages. For instance, a young family may only have a need for protection of income and college funding. Then, later, the family may begin to consider their retirement needs. After the initial plan is implemented, the consumer can plan for the next stage to be implemented, until the entire plan is addressed. Over the years, the life insurance agent would be available to review and adjust the plan periodically, per the changes that the family would experience.

Life insurance is a topic which most people would like to avoid, but most people need to consider protecting the family in the event of an untimely death of a husband or wife. Although most Americans agree that it is important to carry a life insurance policy, many people either lack adequate coverage or simply do not have life insurance on themselves.

Many people have not spoken to a life insurance agent about their financial security. Some do not believe they can afford it and some think it is pre-mature to talk about death. Unfortunately, we cannot predict when we will expire, but we can prepare for the family to continue their lifestyles, if something does happen to us.

Everyday people die of illnesses, health problems, disease, accidents, and murder. There is terrorism, natural disasters such as storms, and earthquakes, and mass murders. Currently, we are at risk for experiencing any of these things at any time.

Our incomes are important to our loved ones. They would not be able to continue their lifestyles without it. Our spouses would have to adjust to be able to pay the bills and to put food on the table. The spouse may have to sell the house or take on a second job. This is precisely what happened to some families which emigrated to the United States and failed to purchase life insurance.

It is just as important to protect a business because the family will suffer if the business owner dies unexpectedly. If there is not enough provision to continue the normal lifestyle, the family will be forced to live below it. Someone must continue running the business so that the family can survive. There must be a plan in place to continue business operations which will be an added expense because the business owner may be difficult to replace.

Life insurance will provide the protection that the family needs. For a very small price, one could purchase a large life insurance policy and have peace of mind knowing that the family is protected. Certain changes in life often trigger the need to purchase life insurance. They include marriage, the birth of a baby, and the purchase of a home. These three events require protection of the income in the event of the death of a spouse. A life insurance agent could assist one in determining how much protection one needs.

Having a life insurance plan to protect the family and a business in the event of the untimely death of one or both parents is wise.

Life insurance is a product which few consumers understand. Therefore, it is beneficial to have a competent life insurance agent for support in making a wise decision to protect the family or business.

Approximately 95 million people are without life insurance protection which means that their families are at risk for financial calamity due to the untimely death of a head of the household. Many families today are headed by a single parent which would leave the family even more at risk. If the parent dies, prematurely, the children would be orphaned. Therefore, single parents need to consider who they would appoint as a guardian to the children. They would also need to provide an income to raise the children. Many families today are ill-equipped to assume the responsibility of one or more children in addition to the family which they may already have. Therefore, the best way to provide an income would be to purchase life insurance.

Typically, employees opt to acquire life insurance at a group rate at work for themselves and for the family, because it is inexpensive. Paying for life insurance weekly or bi-weekly seems to be more feasible for most employees. They can also purchase a separate life insurance policy from an insurance agent outside of work. In this case, employees must determine how long the life insurance will cover them and if the policy is portable, i.e., if coverage remains in force if the employee retires or leaves the company.

Employees would be wise to purchase a separate policy away from work to ensure there is life insurance coverage during gaps in employment or when the employee retires. Some life insurance policies will reduce coverage upon retirement, and some policies are not portable. These are all questions which employees should be asking their life insurance agent to investigate while they are considering purchasing life insurance protection. Consumers should review their life insurance every two years to ensure there is adequate protection for the family in the event of the premature death of the head of household.

Countless people have discovered, when it was too late, that their life insurance policy was inadequate to pay for final expenses or to protect the family. A benefits counselor can help your employees with their decisions about protecting their income for their families.

This financial needs analysis is usually conducted in upper middle class or wealthy individuals. The lower income families do not plan their financial futures. That is why they are poor or living above their means. Most likely, their parents did not plan their financial security, either. It may be a challenge to explain to a member of this class why it is important to have a financial needs analysis done. If the life insurance agent explains things properly, the client should understand why this is necessary.

It is very important for the poor to have life insurance and to consider where they would want their children to be upon their untimely death. If they do not purchase the life insurance on themselves, someone in the family would have to provide burial expenses for the deceased. This would result in undue stress on the family as well as resentment at having to pay for burial expenses because a family member failed to plan.

The reason why many people, including the poor do not purchase life insurance is because of the perceived price. They feel life insurance is too expensive. However, life insurance costs only pennies on the dollar. The policyholder's premiums never total the full value of the death benefit. Upon the death of the policyholder, the beneficiary would receive the full value of the death benefit, regardless of how much the policyholder paid into the policy. The death benefit is guaranteed if the premiums are paid every month.

If consumers, especially the poor, do not designate a guardian for the children, they would become wards of the state upon the death of their parents. Then the state would decide where the children should live.

Many people do not like the idea of paying monthly for life insurance and not receiving any money in return. But this is how life insurance is set up. Policyholders do not receive any of the death benefit while they are alive, unless they borrow a portion of the death benefit. Then they would have to pay it back or it is deducted from the death benefit before the beneficiary collects the death benefit.

The poor person needs a financial needs evaluation done to determine how much money the need to live on and how much they need for final expenses. Even though they only have a small amount of money to work with, they may accumulate more money because they are keeping track of the money and planning for the future.

Anyone can have a financial needs analysis done. It does not matter how much or how little money one has. It is an eye opener as far as determining where the money goes after the check is cashed.

The age of the individual is very important as the financial expert will need to determine how much money the consumer needs to live on in the future and how long it will take him/her to accumulate the amount of money that they need. Then they would have to determine if they can afford to save this amount of money each month.

The client and the financial expert would make a list of all the expenses in the house, as well as all the income earned by each family member. Then they would list all life insurance policies in the family to determine if the policies are adequate, need changes, or need additional policies purchased.

Life insurance is the best ways to protect the family from catastrophe, if one or both heads of the household were to die. Most people cannot afford to accumulate enough money to pay off bills to cover this kind of loss. Fortunately, they can purchase enough life insurance to cover the debt, including a mortgage, that would have been left to the family, had there been no life insurance. The head of household can purchase a substantial amount of insurance for a relatively low cost.

Unfortunately, life insurance is not a priority in the lives of many young families, as younger people tend to believe that they have many years ahead of them. However, the prudent thing to do would be to purchase life insurance to cover a loss of income in the event of premature death of one or both parents or if one of them becomes disabled.

Newlyweds should consider buying life insurance on themselves to protect their incomes if something happens to them. If husband and wife are working, both can purchase life insurance on themselves. In this way, both can continue their normal lifestyles in the event of death or disability of the spouse. Purchasing life insurance in the early years will save money the couple, as the price of life insurance increases as we get older.

When couples purchase a home, they should consider purchasing mortgage insurance to cover the mortgage in the event of death or disability of one of the partners. Many people suffered a loss of their properties during the economic crisis because they were not adequately insured. Some people may not be able to purchase enough life insurance to cover the entire mortgage, but any amount which they can afford now would help their family. They can purchase more life insurance as their incomes increase.

When families experience financial hardship, the insurance is usually the first expense which couples eliminate from their budgets. With the new changes insurance companies have instituted, families can now continue their life insurance coverage if the policyholder is disabled, unemployed, or when the family suffers a natural disaster.

The reason consumers purchase life insurance is to protect one's income. Generally, a couple needs to decide how much money the family is going to need upon their death. The first thing to do is to make a list of all current debts. Then compute the dollar amount of the salary times the number of years parents would like to provide for the family. Add a percentage each year for inflation, as the cost of living increases every year.

For example, John and Mary have $50,000 in credit card debt and an outstanding mortgage of $250,000. John earns $50,000 per year and they decide to include five percent for inflation. Mary would like an income for at least three years after John's death.

Therefore, they would purchase life insurance in the amount of $250,000 + $50,000 (credit card debt) + $150,000 (to cover John's income), which computes to $450,000. Adding five percent for inflation ($22,500) computes to $472,500. This would be the amount of life insurance they would purchase on John.

Most families would elect to cover, at least, the mortgage with life insurance so that the family would not lose the home. The spouse could elect to use the life insurance proceeds to pay off the mortgage upon death of the other spouse or continue paying a monthly mortgage bill. Families need more life insurance when there are under-aged children living in the household.

Ideally, both spouses should purchase an amount of life insurance on themselves to cover the mortgage, if both make contributions from their salaries to pay the mortgage. A life insurance agent can assist in helping the couple to determine the amount of coverage they can purchase, based on their budget.

The most economical insurance policy would be term life insurance, which provides a death benefit without cash value. The most advantageous policy would cover them for ten, fifteen, twenty, twenty-five, or thirty years at a level death benefit. The insurance companies carry different types of term policies for different periods of coverage.

The consumer should ensure that the company they are working with will have a policy which would cover their needs. The spouses would name each other as beneficiaries on each other's policy. In this way, each would collect the proceeds of the policy on the other, upon death.

Younger couples would be able to purchase this amount of coverage very inexpensively. However, older couples would have to pay more money, especially if they have health problems, because the policy premiums increase with age and health conditions. Therefore, they may have to elect lower levels of coverage initially. However, a lower amount of insurance is better than none. Couples should purchase as much insurance as their budgets will allow.

There are three types of term life insurance policies available: the level term policy, the decreasing term policy, and the annually increasing term policy. As previously stated, the term life insurance policy does not have cash value. The consumer would not be able to borrow against the policy in the event of an emergency. The beneficiary would only collect the death benefit upon the death of the insured.

For a level term policy, the death benefit remains the same throughout the term. For instance, if a consumer purchased a thirty - year level term policy in the amount of $100,000 to over a 30 - year mortgage, the beneficiary would collect a death benefit equal to the amount of $100,000. He/she would only collect the death proceeds if the policyholder died during the thirty- year term.

The benefit amount would not increase or decrease during the thirty years that the policy is in force, nor would the premium increase during that time. However, if the policy holder wants to keep the policy in force after the thirty years, the premiums would increase substantially. Most people just let the coverage run out at the end of the term and cancel the policy or convert the policy to a whole life policy before the coverage expires, to cover the parent for the rest of his/her life.

A thirty - year decreasing term policy for $100,000, would be in force for the thirty years, however, the coverage would decrease in increments over the years, according to the outstanding balance on the mortgage each year. The premium would remain the same, throughout the term period. At the end of the ten years, the coverage would be reduced to zero and there would be no more coverage for a death benefit.

The annually increasing term policy, designed to increase with inflation, is rarely used today. The premium increases each year. At some point in the future, most families would not be able to afford to pay the premiums on this policy. However, the policy could be converted to a whole life policy to keep the premiums level and to have the coverage for the rest of the policyholder's life.

With any of these term policies, the policyholder has the option of converting the term life policy to a whole life policy, any time after the first year, to have the permanent coverage. This would include a death benefit that would last until age 100 and a cash value which the policy holder would be able to borrow against in the event of an emergency. The premium would be higher than the term life policy, but it would remain the same throughout the life of the policy.

Whenever a policyholder decides to allow a new life insurance agent to review their whole life policies, they will sometimes compare the current policy with an illustration from their own company to determine which has better cash value. If he/she should show a policy with better cash values, the consumer should be very careful not to put much emphasis on this illustration, because it is not guaranteed and therefore, not an accurate picture of future values. They could fluctuate because they are based on current values.

In most cases, it is not advisable to cancel a whole life insurance policy for another of the same value just because of price. A consumer risks losing the cash value which he/she has built up, in the policy over the years, with their own money. When the consumer does purchase another policy, they would have to start all over again to build up the cash value. If there is a need for the consumer to borrow against the cash value, they would have to wait several years for it to accumulate.

The way to make wise use of cash value in a life insurance policy would be to take a portion of the death benefit in advance in the event a person becomes terminally ill with twelve months to live or less. This would be a better way to make use of a death benefit, as the policyholder would need the funds at this point in their lives.

Most life insurance policies now have this provision, but the terms of the dispersant may vary.

If the policyholder has been diagnosed as terminally ill or with cancer, with twelve months or less to live, he/she can take an advance of up to twenty-five thousand dollars to fifty thousand dollars, depending on the insurance company, to cover his/her expenses. He/she may spend the money any way they desire. Upon the person's death, the beneficiary would receive the balance owed on the death benefit.

Each insurance company has their own rules relative to the amount of advance that can be taken and the length of time the policyholder must be declared terminally ill. This is an option that the policyholder could elect to take. It is not a mandatory+ benefit for the insured. He/she can use the benefit or the beneficiary can take the entire death benefit upon the death of the policyholder.

Couples should decide to exercise this option when making plans for their financial security for the family in the event of the untimely death of one or both spouses.

It is important for families to designate a place to store important documents such as the life insurance policy. I have personally visited a few of the policyholders for my company, only to discover that the policy had been lost because the insured could not remember where they placed it.

When the policyholder expires and the family cannot locate the life insurance policy, they may not be aware that there is a policy or may not be inclined to call the company to inquire about coverage. As a rule, most life insurance companies will not contact the family to notify them that a policy is available upon a person's death. The insurance company does not keep abreast of the deaths of their policy holders.

It is also important to designate the person who will call the life insurance company to report the death and who knows where the policy may be. The person designated to call the life insurance company does not have to be the beneficiary. Nor does the insured have an obligation to tell the beneficiary that he/she has been named as the beneficiary. All the life insurance policies should be stored together.

The insured can store the policies in a folder, in a manila envelope, in a storage bin, file holder, or a safe deposit box at the bank. They can store envelopes or folders in a drawer. The banks would charge a fee for the insured to rent a safe deposit box. Someone in the family should have a key or know where the key is located. The person should also know where and how the life insurance is being stored.

The policy holder can request a copy of the policy or a certificate of insurance from the insurer, if the policy is lost. Some insurance companies charge for a copy of the policy certificate.

If the policyholder should die without telling someone they have purchased life insurance, the life insurance proceeds would never reach the family. It is the family's responsibility to report a death to the insurance company to collect the proceeds.

If the family cannot locate a policy, but remembers that a life insurance agent used to come to the house to collect the premium, there is an agency that the family can contact to determine what company insured the family member for life insurance.

The National Association of Insurance Commissioners has a Life Insurance Policy Locators Service which will assist a consumer who has reason to believe that a deceased family member carried life insurance. A family member can go on-line and answer several questions which will be submitted to participating companies. The companies would then conduct a search of their records for the policy.

Chapter Four

Budgeting for Life Insurance

The biggest problem facing Christian families today is in managing the household budget. Americans have been very irresponsible in managing their money because of their dependence on credit cards. Credit cards have been in use since the 1960's. Those who use credit cards have developed a consciousness of financial illiteracy, though they may not be financially literate.

The average household has about $11,000 in credit card debt. Few know how to reduce their debt or are willing to take responsibility for it. Working class families have too few dollars to handle their household debt. Therefore, they borrow money to pay for their living expenses. Hence, they live beyond their means. Because they are spending most or all their money on consumption, they have little or no money to save for the future. They have the highest percentage of debt and the lowest percentage of savings. They tend to be impulse shoppers, relying on credit cards to make purchases which they cannot afford to pay in cash.

Statement of Need.

If working class Christians truly want to reduce or eliminate their debt, they need to know why they are in debt and what they can do to eliminate it. Most people in the United States are financially illiterate or irresponsible in financial matters, which is the reason for the high level of debt in the country.

Few are aware of sound financial principles and few seek help with their finances. The Bible contains sound financial principles laid down by the Lord, which God expects every Christian to follow. Therefore, a following the Bible-in learning how to manage finances would help Christians in knowing what God expects of them.

Luke 14:28-30 says,"For which of you, intending to build a tower, does not sit down first and count the cost, whether he has enough to finish it – lest, after he has laid his foundation, and is not able to finish, all who see it begin to mock him, saying, " 'This man began to build and was not able to finish?' "

Jesus here advises that we do not spend money unless we already know what it will cost. Then once we determine the cost, we should not go ahead with the purchase, unless we have enough money to buy what we need and what we want. In other words, we should stay within our means, not live over it.

Since many have already experienced miracles in their lives because of being in a relationship with the Lord, they will understand why they need to be obedient in this aspect of their lives as well as how to be good financial stewards of what God has entrusted to them. Doing so will bring them into God's blessings.

Luke 6:10, 11 says, "He that is faithful in that which is least is faithful also in much: and he that is unjust in the least is unjust also in much. If therefore ye have not been faithful in the unrighteous mammon, who will commit to your trust the true riches?" These two verses are very important for those who are handling money. God will only give us responsibility for what we can handle. If we are responsible enough to handle only a little money, then that is what we will get.

However, if we show God that we can responsibly manage more money, he will give us more to manage. If we keep going over our budget, God will not give us more money to handle. We must rectify any amount that we go over before spending any more money. We can go out and get another job or sell something to make up for what we overspend. 2 Thessalonians 3:10 says, "For even when we were with you, we commanded you this: If anyone will not work, neither shall he eat." If we fail to bring in enough money or refuse to work, we will not have enough money even to eat.

If we have a habit of overspending, sooner or later, we will accumulate debt which we are not able to quickly payoff, making it harder for us to spend more money, accumulate more, and take on more responsibility. The solution to this problem is to tithe ten percent of our earnings to the church. In this way, God will make sure we have enough to live on and do the work which he has called us to do. Proverbs 3:9, 10 says, "Honour the Lord with thy substance, and with the firstfruits of all thine increase. So, shall thy barns be filled with plenty, and they presses shall burst out with new wine."

"Honour the Lord" here means to give to the Lord. "Firstfruits" means the first ten percent. We should always put God first. As soon as we cash our paychecks, we should put aside the ten percent of the gross amount that we will tithe to the church, because that is the firstfruits. Then bring it into church and place it in the offering plate. If we do this, "Our barns will be filled with plenty." We will have an abundance of everything we need, including food, clothing, and a place to live.

Psalm 23 says. "The Lord is my shepherd, I shall not want. He maketh me to lie down in green pastures. He leadeth me beside the still waters." If we follow the Lord's leading, we will have enough for our needs. He will not lead us astray and we will have peace of mind knowing that our needs are being met and that we are protected.

It is no secret that the United States is heavily in debt. We have about $11.32 trillion in debt, with about $1.2 trillion of that debt due to student debt, $856.8 billion in credit card debt, $7.92 trillion in mortgages. Let's face it, we have made some mistakes. We are accustomed to living in debt, and the average person has about $11,000 in credit card debt. One in every three people owes more money on their home than what it is worth.

Because of the economic crisis of 2008, high school graduates are attending two-year community colleges, rather than four - year colleges and universities, because parents cannot afford the expense of a four- year college. We have this debt because we are borrowing too much money and we are not conscientious about paying it back. Well over one million people files for bankruptcy each year. Here are a few things that financial advisors are worried about: http://www.mainstreet.com/article/retirement/what-financial-advisors-are-most-worried-about-2014?puc=yahoo&cm_ven=YAHOO

Why are college costs rising faster than inflation?

College costs have been skyrocketing over the past five years. The average cost for tuition for a student to attend state community college in their state in 2012 was $10, 550, which is a twenty-four percent increase over the last five years. Incidentally, the rate of inflation in 2012 was only two percent. Twenty-six percent of students attending colleges full-time are at community colleges, and they are receiving adequate financial aid to cover their costs. These college costs included tuition, room and board, and food.

On the other hand, the college costs for public four- year colleges have increased by twenty-seven percent, which amounted to $17,860.

Students attending out-of-state schools paid $30, 911, as tuition costs were higher. Only two thirds of the students attending colleges and universities receive financial aid, while the other one third must pay their own costs. While these costs increased, the overall budgets for financial aid did not, leaving students to finance more of their college fees on their own.

The costs for attending private colleges and universities have only increased by thirteen percent over the last five years to $39, 518 per year. Tuition and fees averaged $29,056 and room and board amounted to $10,462. If students were fortunate enough to receive scholarships, they paid an average of $23,040 for their education at these private schools.

Because the number of students attending colleges has increased by twelve percent since 2008, and the states have decreased the amount of their awards for financial aid by a little more than 17 percent, the students have had to assume more of their own costs to attend school. The states are now receiving a subsidy of only $6600 since 2008, as opposed to $9300, which they received prior to 2008. However, increased tuitions costs have only covered about two thirds of the lost subsidies.
http://money.cnn.com/2012/10/24/pf/college/public-college-tuition/

To remain competitive, the more selective colleges and universities have spent money to improve the facilities to make them more attractive to parents who are looking for a quality education for their children. Instead of increasing efficiency, reducing costs, or reallocating funds, they are spending money on upgrading and repairing dormitories to appease the students' needs for technology, such as Internet, WiFi, cable, and privacy, including building bathrooms to accommodate only two students, which are becoming necessary in this Digital Age.

Parents are willing to pay the higher costs so their children will be comfortable. They are motivated to pay for the amenities because there is a very high economic return for children who attend private colleges and universities. Test scores for children who attend these schools have improved over the years, proving that it is worthwhile for parents to send their children to these schools and for the colleges to spend money on improvements. The schools are also spending more money on employee health and insurance premiums.

Salaries for employees at colleges and universities have increased. "From 1997 to 2007 academic presidential pay increased by 35%. In 2009 the highest paid university presidents made almost five million dollars. And that's not all. Bloomberg found that when some university executives stepped down, their exit payments were as much as one to three times their annual salary and bonus." http://finance.yahoo.com/blogs/just-explain-it/just-explain-why-does-college-education-cost-much-171454934.html

http://net.educause.edu/ir/library/pdf/ffp0005s.pdf

When considering sending children to college, parents must do their due diligence in locating the right school for their children at the best possible price. For example, some graduates of two -year technical schools majoring in engineering or math, are earning more than those who attended four- year colleges. http://www.usatoday.com/story/news/nation/2013/09/03/how-higher-education-pays/2755345/

Because the banks were losing money, they tightened up on the credit and started increasing interest rates. In 2009, the interest rates soared to unattainable heights, causing the federal government to step in, in an effort to control the rates the banks were charging, and to protect the consumer. They enacted laws to impose limits on the rates and fees that banks could charge the consumer on their banking accounts and businesses on their credit card processing.

Currently, Americans owe $856.8 billion in credit card debt with the average debt being $15,279 per household. The introduction of credit cards in the 1960's has been the major cause of financial illiteracy in the United States. It has caused the following conditions:

- Decline in personal savings rate - In the 1970's and 1980's Americans were saving about 5-7% of their incomes. That savings rate is now 1-3%. People tend not to save money when they know they can use a credit card to purchase products and services. Additionally, payments on credit cards and consumer loans are so high that it is difficult for poor and middle -class people to make the payments, let alone save money. They cannot afford to save money because housing costs are high and wages have remained stagnant since the economic recession of 2008. Consequently, they are paying for groceries and other needs with credit cards because they lack the cash to pay for them. Most consumers do not even have an emergency account to rely on in times of need.

The poor have become so accustomed to using credit cards as a solution to their money problems, rather than learning how to properly manage their budgets. This causes them to not be able to save money nor pay the high interest payments on their credit cards. They go deeper and deeper into debt.

Because the poor tend to be impulse shoppers, wanting everything now, it is difficult for them to delay their gratification, if they rely on credit cards.

- Increasing cultural acceptance of consumer debt as a normal part of life – Consumers have come to accept the fact that they are in debt these days and few are eager to try to get out of debt. Even though unemployment is high along with consumer debt, consumers continue to spend money when they are confident, at the same rate that they did when they were less optimistic about the economy. Even though there is widespread ignorance about financial literacy, consumers planned to increase their spending at Christmas. Few consumers are willing to seek answers to controlling their spending habits and reducing their debt, even though it is 5.5 percent higher than the debt before the recent recession. They want to do what they want with their money.

- Stagnant wages – Because the wage rates have not changed to keep up with inflation, working class people have less money to spend on food and shelter costs which have increased in the years following the economic crisis. Therefore, they are resorting to credit cards to buy groceries, pay bills, and buy gas. There are four million fewer jobs today than there were in 2008. Many of the people who lost jobs in 2008, are still unemployed. Many returned to lower paying jobs which hurt their budgets. Still, others dropped out of the job market permanently because they became discouraged with the high rates of unemployment.

- Decline in financial literacy – As parents have done a poor job of managing their finances, few are taking steps to correct their mistakes. As a result, children are following in their parent's footsteps. The parent is the only role model for spending habits. Children as young as middle school are often given permission to use the parent's credit card. This is teaching the children at an early age to depend on credit cards rather than saving for purchases. Fewer of the parents are teaching their children how to plan for and manage a budget, because they do not know how to do it themselves.

Teens and college students have developed bad spending habits from watching their parents make mistakes in managing their money. Since teens and parents live at home, their parents would be a role model for their behavior in relation to spending. Teens and college students also learn how to use credit cards from their parents, as many of them have permission to use their parents' credit cards from time to time.

If parents encourage students to use credit cards, they learn at an early age that using credit cards to pay for their purchases when they do not have money is acceptable. The students and teens develop an attitude to use credit cards rather than to save money for larger purchases or to elect not to purchase the item. This is the reason why students and teens are financially illiterate.

http://www.moneymanagement.org/Community/Blogs/Blogging-for-Change/2009/April/FLM-Day-24-Student-spending-habits.aspx?RCTAG=FLM

Only forty percent of the population is saving for retirement. Self-employed people, are not saving enough for retirement which could jeopardize their futures. If they do not save for the future, they could end up working for the rest of their lives. As they grow older, they may not be able to perform the jobs because of their health.

https://www.lifehappens.org/blog/retirement-a-ticking-time-bomb-for-independent-workers/

- Increase in bankruptcies

http://www.americanhistoryusa.com/give-me-liberty-or-give-me-debt-a-history-of-credit-cards/

The main reason why people file for bankruptcy is because of medical bills. This is a problem for consumers and business owners. Most people have health insurance to pay the bills, but, unfortunately, health insurance does not pay all of the bills. The average cost for cancer treatment is $500,000. The average cost of a heart attack is $1,000,000. After the insurance company pays its portion, consumers would have to pay anywhere from $10,000 to 20,000. Most people cannot pay these bills because they failed to save the money if this would happen. The average savings account in the U.S. is only $3000. Most people have no more than $500 in their checking account.

http://www.cbsnews.com/news/how-much-would-a-heart-attack-cost-you/

There seems to be a growing trend of business owners who are not saving money for retirement. This goes hand in hand with the lack of financial literacy in this country. Because of the economic conditions in the United States and the tendency of business owners to reinvest their earnings back into the business, they are not earmarking dollars to be set aside for retirement.

This is a very dangerous practice because if business owners continue to do this, they will not be able to retire, but will have to work during their retirement years. One way of beginning a retirement plan is to purchase a whole life insurance plan. This plan accumulates cash value in the third year of the policy and continues if the policy is in force.

Although the returns may not be as high as investing money, it is a good start for someone who is not saving money on a regular basis, as it is a forced savings plan. Many business owners do not save for retirement because they are planning to sell the company to have retirement funds. This is a very risky decision because when they decide to sell the company, the value may not be what they expected. To reduce expenses, some business owners opt not to take a salary, but a better decision would be to reduce expenses or to lay off staff members so that business owners will have a retirement income.

The problem for consumers is in discipline in saving. Consumers need to develop a plan for saving and abide by it. They need to limit, if not eliminate their use of credit cards. If need be, the consumer would do well to write down the goals for saving and keep it with the bank book. For most people, this will be a very difficult habit to break. People will be reluctant to sacrifice the things they like to spend money on in return for saving money. But discipline is one that must replace irresponsible spending and one can start with a few dollars per week. Ten to twelve percent is a better amount to start with because that is a commitment the consumer may be able to live with. The consumer must have a strong desire to be financially secure and must commit to saving a named sum each week, regardless of what happens in the household. If done properly and in the right amount, it will make the consumer a bit uncomfortable, in the beginning.

Nothing must interfere with the plan to save. We fail to accumulate money because we are not committed to saving a designated sum each week.

Once we have set aside the money, we must make a commitment not to withdraw it until we have reached our goal for accumulating the desired amount of money. There may be circumstances which may make us deviate from saving, to lend to those who ask or to invest in stock or seemingly promising money –making opportunities. But, it is best to resist doing this in the beginning so that we can develop strength in our character, which takes time. In the beginning, we may not recognize an unwise investment.

Here is where the whole life insurance would come into play. The cash value would be available for short term needs, such as emergencies.

Studies have shown that it takes anywhere from a few weeks to sixty-six days to change a habit. Since bad habits develop because of stress and boredom, the bad habit must be replaced with a good habit for change to take effect. There should be a way of eliminating the stress and boredom that caused the bad habit. In the case of dependency on credit cards, consumers need to learn to delay gratification instead of wanting everything now. Our grandparents and parents grew up without credit cards, but many of them saved money to buy homes, cars, and other large purchases. They set goals to save money on a regular basis and were patient enough to reach the goal. It also helped not to have credit cards for impulsive purchases.

Consumers will have to adapt to other forms of behavior to replace the urge to use a credit card or to spend money. Once they change this behavior, they will have to eliminate all distractions which will keep them from the path to a better lifestyle

Seeking to improve the skills that they have will enable consumers to think about ways that they can make money instead of spending it.

The acquired skills will allow the consumer to perform their jobs better, thereby making more money.

One example of someone who changed their circumstances in Darnell Smith, owner of Metro Cities Billboards in Fort Worth, Texas. Darnell was a man who was working at one of the factories during the economic crisis of 2008. He lost his job and became homeless after he lost his family. He found an elderly couple who took him in and he helped them around the house in return. He began working on his idea for a digital billboard which gave birth to his current business. As a result, he has become very successful in marketing programs for businesses. He took advantage of an opportunity to make wise use of his time and found a solution to his problem.
http://www.businessinsider.com/billionaires-who-came-from-nothing-2013-12

Changing a bad habit involves disciplining oneself to adopt a new behavior. It can have a detrimental effect on our attitudes and the relationship with others if we are not achieving our dreams and goals. It could make us depressed, careless, moody, and resentful. As we become disappointed with ourselves, we could lose our focus on the things that we are trying to achieve and we could develop a bad attitude. Because we may not be attuned to why we feel this way, we may become ill and experience a host of other thinking patterns which could undermine our well- being and emotional health. This can also affect our relationships with others as they notice a change in our attitudes and we have trouble communicating with and enjoying the company of others.
http://www.discipleshiptools.org/apps/articles/default.asp?articleid=37145&columnid=4166

This inability to control our emotions and feelings of inadequacy stems from a problem with the lack of knowledge and skill in implementing changes in our lives. But most of the people who experience these feelings either do not know why they feel this way, or do not know how to change their lives. They have not discovered the solution to the problem. Consequently, many people go through life never discovering the solution.

The solution is to work diligently whether we see progress or not, as this will help us to achieve our goals. We must work hard every day, as this results in rewards which we had not anticipated. Each step that we take will brings us closer to a successful outcome. The person who has never worked diligently will find it difficult to do so, in the beginning. It helps to have someone to whom to be accountable, who can encourage us to stay on the right path and to endure, even when we do not see immediate results.

If you have children, have them work on a project as well or ask a spouse or other family member to keep them engaged or entertained until you have completed your assignment for the day. This would help the children understand the importance of establishing priorities.

Our lives have changed because of the introduction of digital products which make our jobs easier. They can be our great friend or our worst enemy. While the Internet contains a wealth of information on just about any topic, there are also places where we can waste useful time. The social networks offer opportunities to engage in the exchange of information with friends, family, and prospects. However, this is wasted time if we do not have a goal as to how we are spending time there. If we are business owners trying to increase our cash flow, we should commit to contacting a pre-determined number of prospects per day, and keep non-work activity to a minimum.

It is very easy to be distracted from productive activity with all the people who are engaging on the social networks. However, it is a great opportunity for prospecting, if we use these networks properly, with a goal in mind and with an attitude to complete the goal. Business owners can post useful information about their businesses daily and then decide on how many people they will engage with per day. This can be discussions about the business or in getting to know others through topics of interest with a goal of making the person a customer. Anything other than this can be considered as wasted time. For this reason, our time spent on the social networks should be budgeted.

 At first the new behavior will feel awkward, and as time goes on, we will be accustomed to performing the new behavior to the point where it feels strange to revert to the old ways. http://newleafandcompany.com/how-long-does-it-take-to-form-a-new-habit/

This also applies to our handling of money. A wise person will not invest his/her money frivolously. If we lose it, we will have to start all over again and we will have lost valuable time in accumulating the money.

It is only when we have accumulated enough money that we may want to lend to someone, but only to a person who has the capacity to repay us. It would not be wise to lend to someone, for instance who does not have a job nor has a history of not paying people back. We can encourage the prospective borrower to look for other ways of meeting his/her need for more money.

In the case of investing in money making opportunities like the stock market or a business venture, we should seek the advice of an expert, such as a reputable stock broker, banker, or business consultant. We should only seek the advice of experts and not our next- door neighbor or family member who has no experience in saving and investing. Nor should we seek the advice of someone who has failed to save or has a history of making bad investments. Many people make poor judgements in choosing to seek advice from people who are not capable of giving it. Our tolerance for lending and investing should be according to what we are able to bear.

When there is an economic crisis, people who mishandle their money will suffer because they will not have enough money to pay for bills. They may lose jobs or may have hours cut. Because they do not save money, they will not have emergency savings to fall back on when they experience the reduction in spendable income.

When we manage our money well, we will have enough money saved for emergencies such as an economic crisis. We will always have enough money to pay for household expenses because we are not living above our means. We will be saving and investing the extra money and will have cash available for our every need. We may have to spend more money in some areas, but we will be disciplined enough to reduce our spending in other areas when we need to do so.

There is security in working for an employer who will pay us a weekly or bi-weekly salary. The salary is at a fixed rate. Therefore, we must learn to budget the amount of money we are receiving.

The people who do not manage money well have a tendency to live day to day. However, they are content with having a job and look forward to retirement. The poor money handlers rarely take chances, because they have so little money to live. However, they often do not know where to begin to manage their money properly.

There are various budgeting tools which consumers can utilize to help plan the budget. They include on-line tools and apps which are available on the search engines and on Google Play. The best application I have seen for budgeting is the Mint (http://www.mint.com). The Budget Tracker is another good tool. (http://www.budgettracker.com) Many of these websites can be found on Google Play as apps which you can add to your iPhone, iPad, iPod, or tablet. Keeping track of finances through these tools is a great way to develop good habits toward managing finances properly. Anyone can use the apps on digital products and tools on the websites, as the tool does all the calculations. We merely enter the numbers.

Initially, it can be very tiring and time consuming to plan for the budget and decide how the money will be spent. However, the rewards are great or those who take the time to plan their budgets. It is even better to plan with a spouse and other family members so that everyone commits to the new lifestyle. Each one should be held accountable so that there are no surprises once changes are made.

While consumers are actively adjusting their budgets, there are some ways of reducing or eliminating expenses in some areas. This will help when the time comes for consumers to consider purchasing life insurance. A recent LIMRA study revealed that many consumers do not consider buying life insurance because they think that the cost of insurance is exorbitant and they have other "more important" financial obligations.

Having life insurance is very important for the financial security of the family. Without it, the family would carry the financial burden of paying for the final expenses of a loved one out of pocket, and would have uncertainty over how they would continue their normal lifestyle without the financial support of the loved one. This misconception about the cost of life insurance causes the family to miss out on having their needs met after a breadwinner passes away.

Because of mistakes in managing money, consumers will elect not to buy life insurance because they do not see the value in pay for an intangible item which, in their eyes, they will need in years to come. They would rather pay a high price in later years, so that they can have the convenience of using money, which should be earmarked to pay for life insurance premiums, today.

http://teremity.wordpress.com/2013/10/02/21-ways-rich-people-think-differently/

http://wwwdaveramsey..com/blog/20-things-the-rich-do-every-day

http://www.utrend.tv/v/9-out-of-10-americans-are-completely-wrong-about-this-mind-blowing-fact/

http://atlantablackstar.com/2014/01/03/10-richest-black-communities-america/

Protection Against Bankruptcy

http://gelise1.wordpress.com/2013/10/06/health-care-reform-affects-women/

Businesses file for bankruptcy because they failed to purchase medical coverage or disability coverage to protect them against losses due to accident, sickness or disability. If their businesses are not profitable, then they cannot pay these extra charges in the event of a catastrophe.

They never planned to set aside money to pay for someone to take charge of the business while they are recuperating from their surgeries or illnesses. Many did not anticipate that they would even develop the sickness, illness, or accident. Approximately 60% of businesses that file for bankruptcy do so because of medical bills.

To alleviate this problem, business owners can purchase a health insurance supplement to their health insurance plan. The U.S. government predicts that household out-of-pocket health care expenses will reach an average of $3,301 per year by 2014; yet, the 2013 Aflac Work Forces Report finds that only 23 percent of workers are saving more money in anticipation of medical expense increases. Read more at http://catoosatimes.com/online_features/health_and_wellness/are-you-ready-for-the-real-cost-of-health-care/article_41d24d3e-e94f-530d-ab8e-ef7731e05bbc.html

Life insurance and a health care supplement will protect you and your family from experiencing financial calamity, if you own a business. Life insurance will protect the family in the event of your death. A health care supplement will keep you in business and will prevent having to file for bankruptcy. Seventy-seven percent of people who file for bankruptcy do so because of medical bills. Although most of them had health insurance, they could not afford to pay the out of pocket expenses which they incurred because of the accident or sickness. A health care supplement will cover out of pocket expenses. When we make plans to cover these losses, our financial future is protected. The family has peace of mind.

One of the reasons why people do not purchase insurance is because they feel they cannot afford it. However, the right life insurance agent will show you ways to purchase a plan which is affordable for you and your family. It is better to have some life insurance than none at all.

Lack of adequate cash flow due to the operation of the business is very common. Business owners need to learn how to engage in sales and marketing practices which will increase their businesses. Sales and marketing are vital to the success of businesses and business owners need to develop plans which will help them to grow the business.

Sources for Emergency Cash

There are four sources which consumers should utilize for emergency cash:

1.   Emergency Savings Account – Everyone should have an emergency cash fund in a savings account at the bank. This would be an account which can be tapped at those times when we really need it. Anyone who is trying to save for the future should make this a priority. This will save any retirement plans or college plans from

being tapped whenever an emergency arises. Once we start dipping into the savings plans, it makes it easier to return to the plans to access the money.

2.   Instead, what we can do is to begin to put away money into an emergency cash fund by opening a separate savings account specifically earmarked for this purpose.   The account will grow little by little. We should strive to save about $3000 which will give us enough to meet an emergency need such as purchasing tires, taking an emergency trip, replacing a dryer or washer or other major appliance, covering a deductible on health ins, or buying new clothing for an event. In this way we would have the money when we need it.

3.   We could also purchase a health insurance supplement which would pay out of pocket expenses on major health loses or unforeseen accidents. This would reimburse us for those expenses not covered by co-payments and deductibles. A health insurance supplement is not very expensive and would give a lot of benefits for very little money.   It is especially beneficial to someone who has a high deductible.

4.   One could also have access to emergency cash by purchasing a whole life insurance policy which accumulates cash value over many years. After about the third year, the policy would start to accumulate cash which would increase over the years. In the event of an emergency, this would be another way for consumers to accumulate cash for emergencies.

The consumer could borrow some of the cash value and pay it back with interest. In this way the policy would still be in force, although the face amount of the policy would be reduced somewhat. The policyholder has the option of paying back the cash sometime during the life of the policy. If it is not paid back, then it would be deducted from the amount of the death benefit when the policyholder collects the death benefit. Paying back the cash value would restore the death benefit.

cash value is available in the policy. The cash value increases every year, unless a policy loan is taken against it.

A policyholder may allow the cash value to accumulate, or he/she may take out a loan against it. The cash value is merely a portion of the death benefit that has been set aside so that the policyholder can use it in the event of an emergency. The policy holder would contact his/her life insurance agent to arrange for a loan against the policy. The company designates the amount that is available for borrowing and the interest rate to pay back the loan.

Circumstances under which it is beneficial to use cash value include, college funding. If a parent needs money to cover tuition costs or books, they can borrow money against the cash value on a life insurance policy at a lower interest rate than if they borrowed the money from a bank. When they repay the money, they are paying back into the life insurance policy, building up the death benefit, rather than paying an institution.

A single mother should purchase enough term life insurance to cover college funding for the children in the event of her untimely death. Since there is only one income, the children would not have another parent to rely on for funding their college costs. Therefore, it would be beneficial for the single mother to purchase as much life insurance protection that she can in the event of her untimely death. This would give her and the family peace of mind. The children would be able to attend college in the event of the untimely death of the parent(s).

Therefore, if the parents estimated the cost of a college education at $30,000 per year, the mother could purchase $120,000 of term life insurance on herself, at a very low cost. If there is more than one child, then we would multiply this number by the number of children.

There is a formula which the colleges use to determine if the student qualifies for financial aid based on the parent's income and assets.

The parent can contribute up to forty-seven percent of her income for college funding. This is called the EFC, Expected Family Contribution.

The parent would complete a needs analysis and the parent's Expected Family Contribution would be subtracted from the total cost of a college education. The higher the cost of the education, the more there is a need for the financial aid. If the EFC is less than the college costs, then the family qualifies for financial aid. If he parent has more than one child attending college, then this ECF is divided equally among all the children. There would be more of a need for financial aid with more than one child attending college and with higher college costs.

There are two methods of computing the EFC, the federal methodology and the institutional methodology. The public and colleges use the federal methodology along with the FAFSA application to determine whether the applicant qualifies for Pell Grants and Stafford student loans.

The more expensive colleges and universities use the institutional methodology which also includes a set of questions in the CSS profile along with the FAFSA to determine if the family needs financial aid. With the CSS, more of the family's EFC would be applied toward the student's needs. Family's with a higher level of income could qualify for financial aid under the institutional methodology. Home equities are limited when considering eligibility and retirement income is not included as income in these calculations.
https://www.forbes.com/sites/barbaramarquand/2015/12/16/life-insurance-fails-as-a-college-savings-plan/#4e13ef2a7e23

If the single mother's income qualifies her for financial aid, then she would have to include this amount in the computations for life insurance she would need to cover the cost of a college education for each of her children.   The single mother would probably qualify for financial aid unless she was independently wealthy.

Since most families that need financial aid for college funding have limited incomes, the term life insurance policy would be the best option. The single mother could apply for a large amount of life insurance to cover college funding. This would be the best option for her.

If the single mother already has a whole life policy that she has had for several years, she could use the cash value to help the children purchase books for the classes. A single mother should be encouraged to purchase life insurance on herself to cover college funding costs as soon as possible.

Term life insurance policies will cover a family for a specified number of years. The most common term policies span for 30 years, 25 years, 20 years, 15 years, 10 years and five years. The single mother would not have to carry the life insurance for the rest of her life, as she would he whole life policy. For instance, if aa single mother has a twelve year old child and wants for purchase a life insurance policy

Chapter Six

Retirement

When you retire you will likely be given an option to receive a higher pension in exchange for allowing the pension to stop when you die. With a life insurance plan, you can eliminate the need for an after-death pension, freeing you to select the higher-pension option.

Read more at http://www.business2community.com/finance/10-reasons-why-we-need-life-insurance-0338738#z3VB2CG1YEYwrIVc.99

A recent poll reports that 47% of respondents say they will work longer than they expected. Those who have $100,000 in their retirement account do not have enough money to retire. http://news.msn.com/us/poll-half-of-older-workers-delay-retirement-plans

Before we continue the discussion about protecting the assets, I would like to discuss how to accumulate them. As we have discussed in the past, we need to be disciplined in accumulating money for retirement or any other reason. We need to set aside money for ourselves on a weekly basis so that we can have an income when we retire. Unfortunately, many of us never learned the importance of saving, nor did we learn how to be disciplined. Social security alone is not enough to retire, but it could be a nice supplement to our retirement account.

We have learned from the many economic crises and depressions that we have experienced in the United States that we need to be more disciplined about saving, and we need to make more sacrifices if we are going to be able to save money for retirement. Because of this lack of discipline, many of the Baby Boomers do not have a retirement plan. Consequently, some will need to work to support themselves during their retirement.

Even so, we should still try to save money in the event of an emergency. The first thing to do is to accumulate an emergency fund in a savings account, approximately $2000 or $3000, in case the car, refrigerator, or washing machine break down, or we must take an unexpected trip somewhere. Charles Farrell in his book, Your Money Ratios – 8 Simple Tools for Financial Security at Every Stage of Life, has developed ratios to determine how much money to save on an ongoing basis for retirement. He recommends saving 12% of your salary per year and accumulating twelve times your annual salary as a retirement fund. After setting aside the emergency fund, we can begin to accumulate retirement money.

A close examination of the budget will reveal where we are spending money and whether we need to adjust the budget to save twelve

percent. By keeping track of money spent and deciding what we can eliminate from our spending, we will find the twelve per cent to move into a retirement pan. We can begin a plan at work, or if self-employed, we should begin a plan on our own, through a bank, or an insurance company.

Once the plan is in place, we should purchase a life insurance plan to cover other expenses, such as estate taxes, final expense benefits, and to maximize the pension. If we elect to take a higher payout from a pension plan, the pension will end upon death. However, we can take out insurance for the amount we will lose because we are taking a higher payout, and ensure the spouse will still have the income upon the death of the other spouse to cover their living expenses.

Another situation where a policy owner could borrow cash value from a life insurance policy would be as a tax -free retirement fund. They could plan for withdrawals or loans to supplement their retirement plan. A retirement specialist could be very helpful in a situation such as this. It would depend on the amount of cash value available and whether the policyholder desires to have a death benefit after all is done.

In conclusion, accumulating money for retirement, and protecting the income with life insurance are wise decisions for those who desire to live comfortably during retirement.

Chapter Seven

Women as Heads of Household – Changing the Tide

It is important to protect the children through life insurance in the event that the parents pass away before the children reach the age of majority. The main reason why insurance companies advise parents to buy life insurance is because of the need to provide for the children if they should pass away prematurely.

Parents provide a lot of resources for the family, including food, shelter, clothing, schooling, health benefits and recreation for the children. It is estimated that the parents will spend:

Dual-Parent Family

Age of Child	Housing	Food	Transportation	Clothing	Health	Child care /Education	Miscellaneous	Total
Before-tax income: Less than $59,410 (Average = $38,000)								
0 to 2	2,990	1,160	1,170	640	630	2,040	420	9,050
3 to 5	2,990	1,260	1,230	500	590	1,910	620	9,100
6 to 8	2,990	1,710	1,350	570	660	850	630	8,760
9 to 11	2,990	1,970	1,350	580	710	1,290	630	9,520
12 to 14	2,990	2,130	1,480	690	1,090	880	700	9,960
15 to 17	2,990	2,120	1,630	730	1,010	910	580	9,970
Total	53,820	31,050	24,630	11,130	14,070	23,640	10,740	169,080
Before-tax income: $59,410 to $102,870 (Average = $79,940)								
0 to 2	3,920	1,405	1,690	760	850	2,860	890	12,370
3 to 5	3,920	1,490	1,740	610	800	2,740	1,090	12,390
6 to 8	3,920	2,100	1,860	680	940	1,680	1,110	12,290

9 to 11	3,920	2,400	1,870	710	1,000	2,110	1,100
	13,110						
12 to 14		3,920	2,580	1,990	840	1,410	1,910	1,170
	13,820						
15 to 17		3,920	2,570	2,150	900	1,330	2,400	1,050
	14,320						
Total	70,560	37,620	33,900	13,500	18,990	41,100	19,230
	234,900						

Before-tax income: More than $102,870 (Average = $180,040)

0 to 2	7,100	1,900	2,550	1,050	980	5,090	1,790
	20,460						
3 to 5	7,100	2,000	2,610	880	930	4,970	1,990
	20,480						
6 to 8	7,100	2,630	2,730	970	1,080	3,910	2,000
	20,420						
9 to 11	7,100	2,980	2,730	1,010	1,150	4,350	2,000
	21,320						
12 to 14		7,100	3,190	2,860	1,170	1,610	4,700	2,070
	22,700						
15 to 17		7,100	3,180	3,020	1,280	1,520	6,460	1,950
	24,510						
Total	127,800		47,640	49,500	19,080	21,810	88,440
	35,400	389,670					

If you have been reading my postings on my fan page or my my blog, you may have drawn a conclusion that you need to purchase life insurance.

The reason we purchase life insurance is to protect one's income. Generally, we need to decide how much money the family is going to need upon our death. The first thing to do is to make a list of all debts that you have now. Then compute the dollar amount of your salary times the number of years you would like to provide for the family. Add a percentage each year for inflation, as the cost of living increases every year.

For example, John and Mary have $50,000 in credit card debt and an outstanding mortgage of $250,000. John earns $50,000 per year and they decide to include 5% for inflation per year. Mary would like an income for at least three years after John's death.

Most families would elect to cover, at least, the mortgage with life insurance so that the family would not lose the home. The spouse could elect to use the life insurance proceeds to pay off the mortgage upon death of the other spouse.

Ideally, both spouses should purchase an amount of life insurance on themselves to cover the mortgage, since both make contributions from their salaries to pay the mortgage. A life insurance agent can assist in helping the couple to determine the amount of cover they can purchase, based on their budget.

The most economical insurance policy would be term insurance which provides a death benefit without cash value. The most advantageous policy would cover them for ten, twenty, or thirty years at a level death benefit. The spouses would name each other as beneficiaries on each other's policy. In this way, each would collect the proceeds of the policy, if the other dies.

Younger couples would be able to purchase this amount of coverage very inexpensively. However, older couples would have to pay more money, especially if they have health problems. Therefore, they may have to elect lower levels of coverage. However, a lower amount of insurance is better than none. Couples should purchase as much insurance as their budgets will allow.

In conclusion, couples should make plans for their financial security for the family in the event of the untimely death of one or both the spouses.

Watching the Olympics may inspire those of us with an adventurous spirit to venture off into another country to pursue a dream of mountain climbing in a place like Mt. Kilimanjaro in Tanzania.

Only those who are accustomed to walking or climbing long distances on arduous paths would be capable of under taking such an adventure. Mt Kilimanjaro has been the subject of a few suspense novels and motion pictures over the years and could inspire someone to visit this picturesque area.

Although no one would ever dream of experiencing a mishap while traveling, it would be a good idea to include insurance protection in the event of a unforeseen accident when we may travel. Just as we plan our financial security by purchasing life insurance, we need to consider an accidental death policy to plan for those times where we may have an accident while traveling.

Accidental death or double indemnity benefits can be purchased as an individual policy or as a rider on a life insurance policy. Purchased as a rider, the covered person is insured in the event he/she dies because of an accident.

The benefits payable would be twice the amount of the face value of the life insurance policy. For instance, if a person has a $25,000 life insurance policy, and a rider for the accidental death benefit, the beneficiary would collect $50,000 if the covered person dies because of an accident. Some insurance companies have a provision where the covered person can elect the amount of the death benefit in multiples of $5000, not to exceed the face amount of the policy.

When the accidental death indemnity policy is a separate policy, the benefits are more inclusive. There is a provision in most policies for medical and other expenses incurred in the accident. However, certain types of activities may be excluded. Depending on the need, it would be worthwhile to investigate these policies.

In conclusion, it would be wise to purchase an accidental death policy before traveling on vacation or on assignment.

Perhaps one of the most sensitive issues in managing a life insurance policy is in choosing beneficiaries. If we have been responsible enough to buy life insurance, we must also be responsible enough to appoint the best person to collect the proceeds, use it wisely, and fulfill our wishes as to how the proceeds should be spent.

One of the benefits of life insurance proceeds is that they can be collected with having to be probated. The beneficiary simply notifies the life insurance company of the death of the policyholder, and the insurance company processes the claim. A check is then issued to the beneficiary within a few days to a few weeks, after the insurance company has determined that the beneficiary has a right of claim per the terms of the insurance contract.

If the policy being considered is to pay the final expenses of a burial, a spouse should be named as the beneficiary, since, he or she will be the one to make the funeral arrangements. Usually one beneficiary is needed, but the policyholder can name a contingent beneficiary, if the beneficiary dies before the policyholder has a chance to name another, or if both the policyholder and the beneficiary were to die together in an accident. The policyholder can change the name of the beneficiaries as often as he/she feels necessary.

For larger policies, which are being created to fund a trust or to give money to multiple members of the family, the policyholder can name more than one beneficiary along with the percentage of the proceeds to which each has been assigned. In this way, the proceeds can be collected without having to go to probate and the proceeds are tax free.

It is important to choose a beneficiary wisely as this is going to be the person who will carry out your wishes. If you decide to tell the person you have chosen to be a beneficiary, it would be wise to make it clear how the money will be spent. It is also wise to have a will which will detail your wishes for the settlement of your estate. Many people have disputed the settlement of estates and the decisions as outlined in a will.

If a policyholder does not have a next of kin or does not wish to name a beneficiary from the family, he/she can name his/her estate as the beneficiary. In this way, when the estate is settled, the probate judge will disperse the funds at his own discretion. As it takes two or three years to settle an estate, or maybe longer, the family should wait for the probate judge to decide. This could interfere with the funeral arrangements if there exists no other insurance or proceeds to pay these expenses. Therefore, a life insurance is necessary for the payment of final expenses.

The probate laws for each state are different and it is important for all the involved parties to know how the laws are interpreted. If there are questions, a lawyer can help ensure that the family follows the laws of the state and the instructions outlined in the will.

Chapter Eight

The Needs of Divorced Women

How do you pay for life insurance if you are really living on a tight budget? Many people such as divorced women with children claim they cannot afford to pay for life insurance. However, if one works closely with your agent, he/she can find a policy which you can afford.

The term life insurance policy is the least expensive policy because it is only designed to cover temporary needs for life insurance, at a low cost, such as when the mortgage paid or other short- term debts are paid off. It usually spans from 5, 20, 25, or 30 years and then the premium increases dramatically. The policy holder can convert the insurance to a permanent whole life policy after the first year of the policy, if want to continue the policy beyond the term period. The premium will be higher at that point.

If you desire to purchase life insurance and cannot afford the price of permanent insurance, you can purchase term and then convert it when your financial situation improves. Your life insurance agent will generally follow up with you one year after the policy is sold to determine if it would be appropriate to convert the policy.

Here are some things you can do to reduce the budget:

1.   Some people do not want to give up their entertainment and arts events. In this instance, be on the lookout for savings on tickets or even free tickets in the newspapers. Also, some places allow you to be an usher at the event, where you can view the show, or movie for free. I did this recently at a cinema in Providence. They needed someone to hand out and collect completed surveys during the movie. I saw the movie for free.

If you become a member of an arts organization, sometimes they allow you to attend their events for free or at a reduced price. The local NPR also gives access to free events, if you become a member. Check the organizations you like and see what they have to offer.

2.   If you like to travel, an AAA membership comes in handy. There are coupons for valuable savings at different hotels, restaurants, and events. Always check before you go on a trip. You could save hundreds of dollars. This could be applied to your life insurance policy.

If you are willing to travel off season, you can reserve some accommodations at lower off seasons rates. Some hotels offer memberships in frequent stayers' clubs where members can receive bargains on rates on hotel fees. Call around to the hotels in the area where you planning to visit and ask for these rates. It may take time to find an affordable rate, but the savings will be well worth it.

3.   For electronics purchases, you can go to Overstock.com for deals on purchases. Also, some manufacturers will sell refurbished or "open box returns" at a lower price. Ask when you talk to them about a purchase. You can also ask about refurbished appliances at places like Sears.

4.   If you like to eat out, look for coupons in the local newspaper two- for-one at restaurants and look for restaurants who are registered on Retaurant.com. They give gift certificates for meals at reduced prices. Also, try growing your own vegetables in the summer instead of buying them.

So, here are a few ideas to keep costs down. What you save can help pay for a much-needed life insurance policy.

Chapter Nine

The Needs of Single Women

Many single people are under the impression that they do not need life insurance, however, even though they do not have dependents, they may have someone in their life who is dependent on them for support.

For instance, some single people may have purchased a piece of property jointly with someone else. Often, people who co-habitate may decide to buy a house together. In this instance, if both are contributing to the mortgage payment, and if one dies, the other would have difficulty making the payments on their own. In this instance, each would need life insurance on the other, naming each other as beneficiaries. This would enable the survivor to continue paying the mortgage, pay final expenses for burial, and living the life style he/she was accustomed to living before the death of the partner.

Life insurance is less expensive in the early years, and therefore, it would be beneficial for single people to purchase life insurance before a decision to marry or have children. If they are helping to support a family member, that family member will miss the support, if the single person were to die.

A single person may not want to leave the family with large debts upon an untimely death, especially if they saw another family member experience hardship because of the loss. Therefore, if they are having outstanding college loans or mortgage payments, and want to leave the family with enough to pay their final expense benefits, they can purchase enough life insurance to cover these debts if they die prematurely.

Finally, life insurance is another way to save money on a tax deferred basis. After three years, the whole life policy would have cash value that the single person could use to begin a retirement plan or college fund. With variable life insurance, they could accumulate higher amounts of cash value.

Single mothers and single fathers need to plan for their financial security very carefully. Because there is only one parent, the parent has to give careful consideration as to how the children will consider their normal lifestyle, if something were to happen to the mother or father.

Because the single parent can only rely on one income, it is especially important to open an emergency fund to cover repairs on the automobile, emergency trips, and living expenses due to unforeseen events. This will help in time of need.

It is also important to designate a guardian in the event of the untimely death of the parent and to purchase life insurance to help cover the living expenses for the children. The addition of new family members could put an additional strain on the new family. A will would have to be created which would designate who the guardians will be. If guardians are not appointed, the state would designate someone who would be entrusted with custody of the children.

If the plan is for the children to go to college, the earlier the parent saves money toward this goal, the better. Since the children are relying on one income, parents can accumulate more money in interest. if they start saving early. Additionally, there are state sponsored insurance plans available for the accumulation of college funding.

Some employers offer short-term and/or long term disability plans in the event of sickness or disease. However, the single parents should also consider a separate supplemental disability plan which would offer payments in addition to what the company offers. Often, the plan which is available at work is inadequate to continue paying for household expenses. One can secure a disability plan as a rider on some life insurance plans.

When purchasing health insurance at work, single parents should elect a plan with a low deductible and little or no copayments to protect the income. Since there is only one income, the single parent is more in need of a low deductible so that they can have the extra money for household expenses.

In conclusion, single parents need to be more responsible with their financial planning to ensure their families are protected in the event of emergencies and untimely death of the parent.

Chapter Ten

The Needs of Widows

Unfortunately, many of the men have refused to take responsibility for the family, leaving the women to provide for their children. This makes insurance even more important for the family, since the children would be left without a single parent in the event of the untimely death of the mother.

In this situation, God provided for the widow and her children in asking the owners of vineyards to leave the sheaves that were left in the field for the widows and orphans. God outlined specific duties regarding gleaning in Deuteronomy 24:20, which states: "When thou beatest thine olive tree, thou shalt not go over the boughs again: it shall be for the stranger, for the fatherless, and for the widow." God explains in verse 22 why the owners of the vineyard should leave the sheaves in the field. He states, "And thou shalt remember that thou wast a bondman in the land of Egypt: therefore, I command thee to do this thing."

This was a way of providing for the poor people in those days. In modern times, the institution of welfare and human services has become a means of support for poor families. However, life insurance is a way in which widows and orphans can continue to lead their normal lifestyles in the event of the death of the head of the household.

Life insurance provides for a lump sum of money to be awarded to the wife so that she can pay the bills and provide for the children. Life insurance is God's answer to the security of the family; therefore, it is wise to seek a life insurance policy to protect the family in the event of the death of one or the other breadwinners.

For the family to be protected, there would have to be a savings account totaling the future expenses in raising the children and caring for them while they are living with the parents. Since most families do not have this amount of money in savings, life insurance is the best solution to this problem.

Chapter 11

Dispersing the Life Insurance Funds

One of the ways in which policyholders can control the dispersing of the life insurance proceeds paid to their beneficiaries is with trust funds. The wealthy classes have used life insurance a s a form of wealth transfer for many years. Instead of using their own cash to transfer wealth to their children or other relatives, they will often purchase large amounts of life insurance and name their family members as beneficiaries. To avoid squandering of the life insurance proceeds, the policy owners would place the life insurance in a trust designating when and how the money is to be dispersed.

In this way. The parent could limit the amount of life insurance coming out of the trust at one time to monthly payments over the life of the individual, to help him/her be more responsible.

If a family desires wealth for their children, they must consider how the money is going to be spent. Parents should not extend the wealth to their children unless they have been properly trained and counselled in how to manage money and they have a plan to use the money. This should be a training that begins in childhood and extends through their early adult years. They should have a good education and should know how to manage money responsibly in their early adult years. The Bible says, in Proverbs 22:6, "Train up a child in the way he should go, and when he is old, he will not depart from it."

This is especially recommended for people who grew up in poor families and have become affluent in their own lifetimes. We have heard of countless stories, for instance, of people who have won the lottery and have become destitute after a time of squandering the money instead of making plans to spend it. Today, people do not need a million dollars to have a trust fund. It can be a large enough sum that you feel would be too large of a sum of money for your child to manage without squandering.

The most attractive feature of purchasing life insurance to transfer wealth to the family is that life insurance can be purchased for "pennies on the dollar." For example, If you purchase a $50,000 whole life insurance policy for $80.00 per month at age 45 and paid it for 30 years until your death, you would have spent $28,800 and your beneficiary would receive $50,000. While you are paying into that life insurance policy, you have access to cash value in the policy for emergencies, but you could capitalize on the policy if you choose to use it for increasing your wealth, such as a down payment on a home, a car, or to invest it into a business.

Chapter 12

Business Insurance

Business partners need a buy-sell agreement or buyout agreement when they form a business or immediately after. It is an agreement which protects the interest of each party whenever there is an event which would change ownership. The agreement would set the price and the conditions upon which the mandatory or optional buyout would take place. Whenever this process is delayed, the business owners increase their financial risk.

The goals of the buy sell agreement would be:

the identification of the events which would trigger the purchase of the business and to ensure that the business owners' interest would be protected,

to identify the buyer of the owner's interest in the business, i.e., the company, the remaining owner, or joint ownership of the owner and the business,

to provide a procedure for determining purchase price of the business, according to market conditions when the event occurs,

to provide a way of funding the agreement, such as through life insurance

to determine the deceased owner' interest in the business for estate tax purposes

There are several events which would trigger the optional buyout of an owner's interest in the business. They include death or disability of an owner, the decision to transfer ownership to a third party, the retirement of an owner, divorce of an owner, or bankruptcy of the business.

In the event of death or disability, the business owner's family would be protected, since the business owner supported the family with his share of the proceeds of the business. If the decision to create a buy sell agreement is delayed, it places the family at risk for financial hardship. Conversely, divorce or bankruptcy would make the business vulnerable to outsiders, such as a spouse or a creditor. Creating a buy-sell agreement would prevent these outsiders from taking over the business.

With many of the insurance products, there usually are not any tax consequences until you start withdrawing money from them. That is why it is important to consult a tax accountant before deciding to withdraw money from these products. Depending on the circumstances, accepting disbursements from life insurance or annuity products could subject the policy owner or beneficiary to paying taxes at the end of the year.

Appendix A

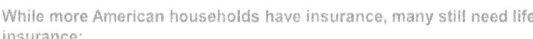

Facts About Life 2016

Facts from LIMRA
Life Insurance Awareness Month, September 2016

While more American households have insurance, many still need life insurance:

- In 2016, there are nearly 5 million more U.S. households that have life insurance coverage, compared with 2010 results. However, 30 percent of households (37.5 million) remain uninsured.

- There are 3.1 million more households with individual life insurance than in 2010, a 6 percent increase from 2010. However, the individual life insurance market penetration remained steady. Only 44 percent of U.S. households have individual life insurance, equal to the 50-year low set in 2010.

- Approximately 50 million households recognize they need more life insurance (40 percent of households).

More Millennials own life insurance

- Overall, 70 percent of Millennials own some life insurance (individual, group or both) - 10 percentage points higher than in 2010. In addition, Millennials' ownership of individual life insurance has increased 48 percent since 2010.

- The top three reasons Millennials own life insurance is to pay for final expenses (funeral, burial, etc.): 49 percent; to replace income: 35 percent; and to pay off mortgage: 22 percent. This aligns with the general population.

- Sixty-five percent of Millennial households say they are likely to buy life insurance within the next 12 months, 29 percentage points higher than in 2010.

- Millennials are as likely to have bought life insurance face-to-face as other age groups but Millennials are more likely to have bought life insurance though other channels as well. The ability to purchase life insurance at their workplace is a plus for Millennials – and improves the likelihood that they will purchase life insurance.

Facts About Life 2016

More households with children under 18 have life insurance

- One and five households with children under age 18 are uninsured in 2016, which is 3.7 million fewer households, compared with 2010 results.

- Of those families who have no life insurance coverage, 73 percent recognize they need life insurance and 62 percent say they would be in immediate financial trouble if a primary wage earner died.

- Two-thirds of the households said they were likely to purchase life insurance within the next 12 months.

Life insurance coverage adequacy has declined – Market need exceeds $12 trillion

- In 2016, there was a significant decline in life insurance coverage adequacy for U.S. households. In 2010, those insured had coverage to replace their income for 3.5 years. Today that has dropped to 3 years, which is far lower than most industry recommendations.

- Across all age groups under 65, the income replacement rate (# of years covered) has declined.

- Using LIMRA's Life Insurance Needs Model, LIMRA estimates that 48 percent of households (60 million) have a life insurance coverage gap of $200,000 on average, which amounts to more than $12 trillion in total market need.

- Among households with children under 18, 4 in 10 say they would immediate financial trouble if a primary wage earner died today.

- Another 3 in 10 would have trouble keeping up with basic living expenses after several months

- Overall, 7 in 10 of all households said they would have trouble covering everyday living expenses after several months if the primary wage earner died.

- Forty-eight percent of households need more life insurance based on LIMRA's need model. That's 60.1 million families. The average need is close to $200,000

Facts About Life 2016

Why don't they buy?

- Eight in 10 households who believe they need more life insurance say they don't buy because of other financial priorities. Or they can't afford it. But prior research shows that, on average, people estimate life insurance to cost three times what it actually does.

- Six in 10 say they don't know what to buy or how much they need. One of the biggest obstacles is lack of information (up 23 percent from 2010).

- More households who believe they need more life insurance say the reason they haven't purchased is because they haven't been approached by a financial professional (25 percent in 2010 vs. 35 percent in 2016).

Reaching Consumers:

- Almost half (45 percent) of U.S. households say they are likely to buy life insurance in the next 12 months; an 80 percent increase from 2010. This is most likely among younger households (under age 45) and married couples with children.

- More than one-third (35 percent) of married couples with dependent children want to speak with a financial professional about their life insurance needs.

- Across all age groups and income levels, insured households said they want to review their life insurance coverage annually. This is significantly higher than in 2010.

- The majority of households said they were more likely to buy when advised by trusted financial professional (56 percent).

All facts are from several of LIMRA's life insurance consumer studies.
Fact sheet may be reproduced in whole or in part if attributed to LIMRA.